SARAH'S CHRISTMAS CROWN

By Marty Grimes

Illustrated by Judy Findley

3G Publishing, Inc.
4495 Atlanta Highway, Suite C28
Loganville, GA 30052
www.3gpublishinginc.com

First published by 3G Publishing, Inc., June, 2020.

Printed in the United States of America

ISBN: 9781941247778

Dedication

To Sarah
Hannah, Benjamin, Nathan, Timothy, Molly,
Elizabeth, Daniel, Elliot, David, Evan, and Robbie
&
Dylan, Clare, Liam, Ella, Adam, Colin, Kate, Austin and Sunny

Sarah's family moved toward their
seats at Grandma and Grandpa's church.
So many people!
"Merry Christmas!" they whispered as
the family moved quickly down the aisle.
"Merry Christmas!"
"Merry Christmas!"
"Merry Christmas!"

5

Sarah shyly smiled at the girl waving from the front row, then looked past her, eyes wide. The church was all dressed up: big red poinsettias, green wreaths on the windows and tall candles on the sills, a beautiful big Christmas tree up front.

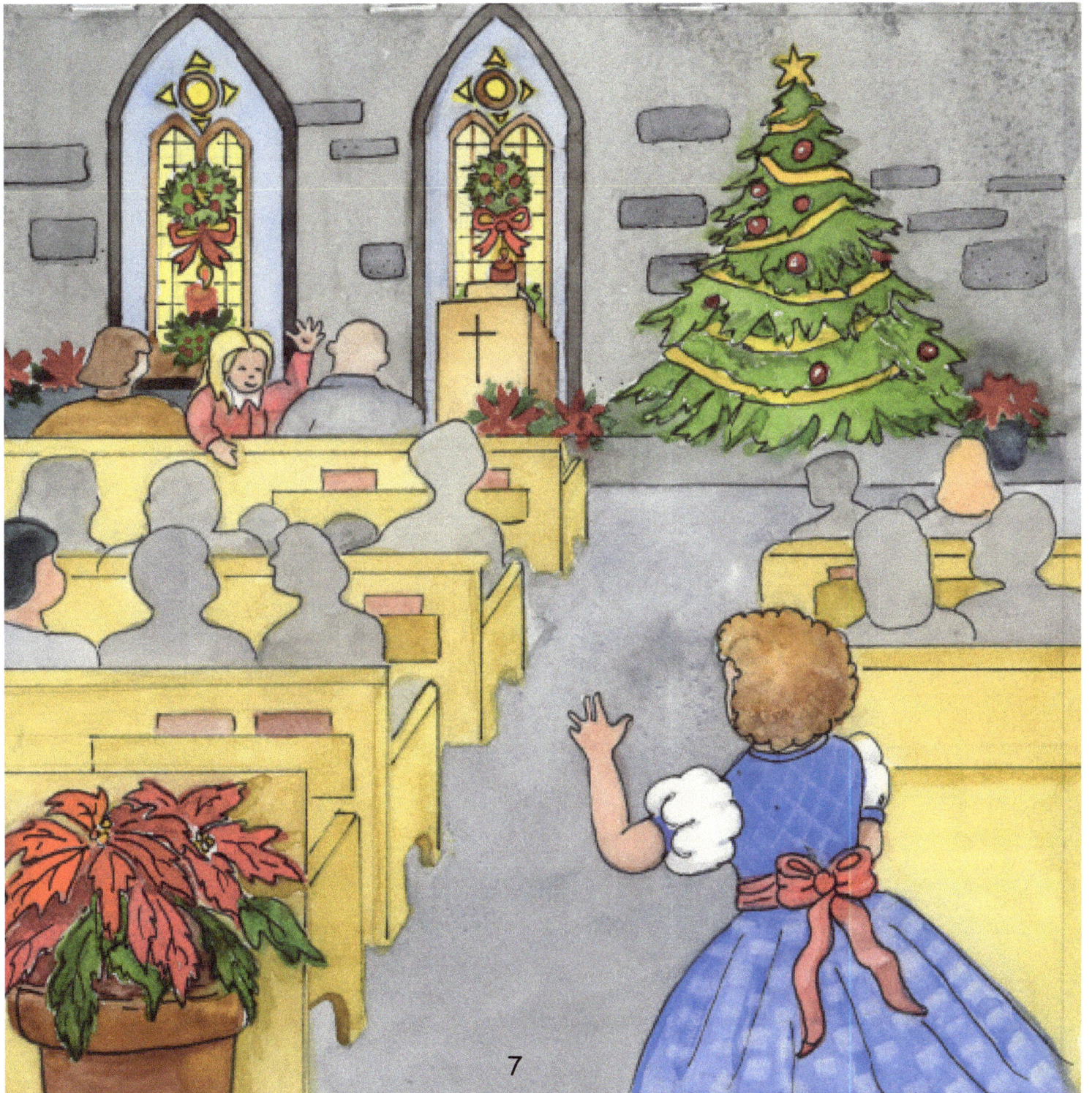

The service was starting. Some of her favorite Christmas music drew her attention and Sarah happily joined in with the singing.

How pretty it all sounded!

Everyone was singing the very songs Mommy had taught her!

Sarah nestled under her Grandma's arm when the music quieted. Now it was time to listen.

Pastor Fred's words caught her attention.
He was telling a story about God's love.
About how God sent His son Jesus to live among
the people here on earth. Jesus would grow up
to show them what God is like and how much
God loves them and wants to be the King of their
lives.

Sarah knew this story.

Christmas is when we remember and celebrate
God's present to us - Jesus! It's our invitation
to be a part of his family, Jesus' family.

Sarah sat very still, not moving a muscle. She loved stories.

With her eyes wide open and her ears catching each word, Sarah heard the minister say,

"When we choose to be part of Jesus' family, we are children of the King!"

Suddenly, Sarah knew that made *her* a princess!

Pastor Fred continued, ***"Can't you just feel the crown on your head?"***

As she listened, Sarah slowly ... expectantly ... raised both hands to the tip top of her head to feel for her crown. And a big smile spread across her face.

Soon, the lights dimmed, and Grandma handed Sarah a small white candle wearing a white paper collar. She stood on the pew when the familiar music of Silent Night began, a dainty circlet of gold perched among the curls on her head.

As the candles were lit, the dancing flames were reflected in Sarah's wide eyes.

Pastor Fred said that the candle light was like the Baby King Jesus. He came to be a light to our world. His light helps us know God and love him.

Sarah looked around the church to see all the candles lifted high, filling the room's darkness with a warm glow. And, Oh! In the light of all those candles, Sarah saw something wonderful!

CROWNS!
Sparkling crowns

on the heads of many of the other people in the room!

What a big family King Jesus has!

As her family left the church at the end of the service, Sarah giggled as Pastor Fred leaned way down to shake her hand. His crown had slipped down the side of his head. He had been doing a lot of hugging and handshaking at the door. He winked at her as he said, "Merry Christmas, Sarah!"

As the family walked to the car, Sarah's small hand was tucked safely in Daddy's big one. Sarah looked back at the church, at the light tumbling out the open door and through the windows into the dark Christmas Eve night. She thought about the baby King Jesus being the light of the world.

Sarah thought happily about being a princess in King Jesus' family - and felt once again ever so carefully toward the top of her head, for her very own Christmas crown.

The Birth of Jesus
Luke 2:1-20 The Holy Bible

About that time Caesar Augustus ordered a census to be taken throughout the Empire. This was the first census when Quirinius was governor of Syria. Everyone had to travel to his own ancestral home-town to be accounted for. So Joseph went from the Galilean town of Nazareth up to Bethlehem in Judah, David's town, for the census. As a descendant of David, he had to go there. He went with Mary, his fiancée, who was pregnant.

While they were there, the time came for her to give birth. She gave birth to a son, her firstborn. She wrapped him in a blanket and laid him in a manger, because there was no room in the hostel.

An Event for Everyone
There were sheepherders camping in the neighborhood. They had set night watches over their sheep. Suddenly, God's angel stood among them and God's glory blazed around them. They were terrified. The angel said, "Don't be afraid. I'm here to announce a great and joyful event that is meant for everybody, worldwide: A Savior has just been born in David's town, a Savior who is Messiah and Master.

This is what you're to look for: a baby wrappped in a blanket and lying in a manger.

At once the angel was joined by a huge angelic choir singing God's praises:

> Glory to God in the heavenly heights,
> Peace to all men and women on earth who please him.

As the angel choir withdrew into heaven, the sheepherders talked it over. "Let's get over to Bethlehem as fast as we can and see for ourselves what God has revealed to us." They left, running, and found Mary and Joseph, and the baby lying in the manger. Seeing was believing. They told everyone they met what the angels had said about this child. All who heard the sheepherders were impressed.

Mary kept all these things to herself, holding them dear, deep within herself. The sheepherders returned and let loose, glorifying and praising God for everything they had heard and seen. It turned out exactly the way they'd been told!

The Message

About the Authors

Marty Grimes, Author
Judy Findley, Illustrator

Marty Grimes is a writer living in Georgia with her husband of almost fifty years; together they raised three children who have added twelve grandchildren to the family. Marty is a Christ follower, a retired school administrator and missionary to Haiti. She loves spending time with her family, and these days can be found writing, taking watercolor art classes, hiking, reading, knitting, kayaking - and considering which grandchild to write about next.

Judy Findley is an Oregon watercolor artist and illustrator whose interests are her family, doing creative things such as knitting, gardening, painting and sketching. She is a member of The Oregon Watercolor Society, Corvallis Art Guild, and Vistas and Vineyards plain-aire painting group. She loves the Lord and was honored to have the opportunity to illustrate this sweet story.

www.ingramcontent.com/pod-product-compliance
Lightning Source LLC
Chambersburg PA
CBHW060801150426

42813CB00058B/2783

9 781941 247778